To . . . .

From . . . . . .

DOGS
a guide to domestic bliss

by James Croft

LAUREL
GLEN

Very broadly speaking,
a dog's life can be expressed
as a simple pie chart.

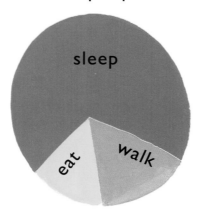

But that would be to ignore all the subtle
nuances that go to make up the complex
and highly organized machine that is...

...a dog's world.

Contents

Essentials

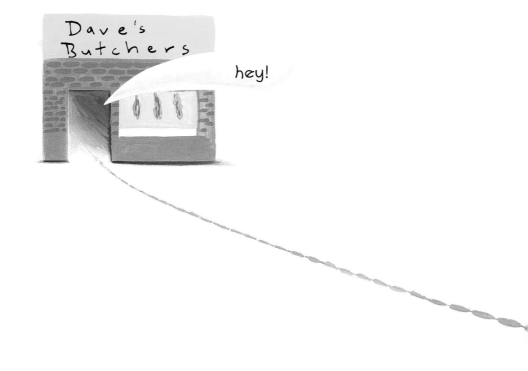

Things I like to eat...

sausages

flies

treats

My favorite walk

Things I like
to chew...

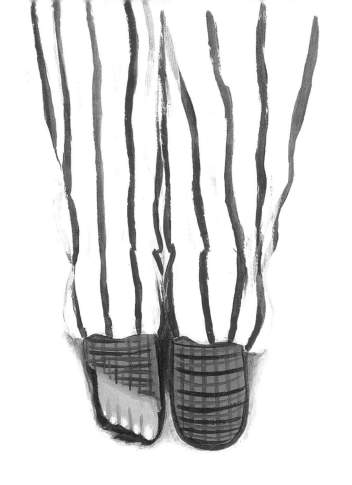

slippers

squeaky toys

Best places
to sleep...

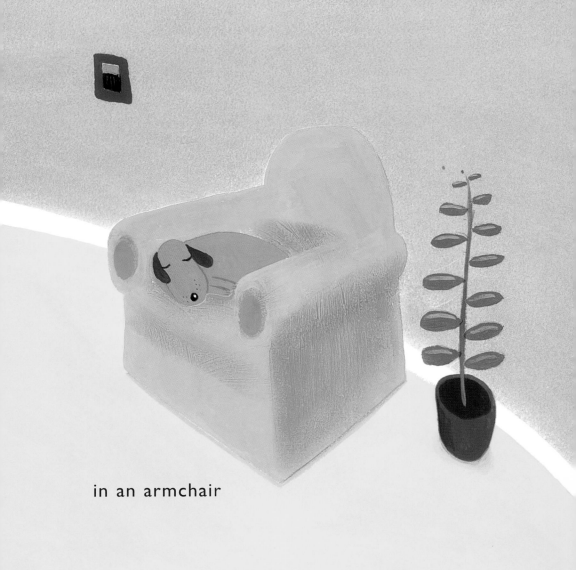

in an armchair

in the sun

My domain

Best Things

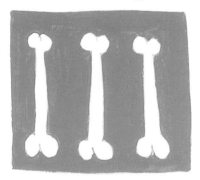

in Life

Digging

I love digging.

Burying

Stretch Armstrong

Sniffer

Rover Two-Tails

Old friends...

Paws
McGinty

special
friends...

She's crazy about me.

new friends

Things that need fetching

stick

ball

Mr. Mouse

big stick

apple

squeaky toy

Travel

Patting

Tickling

Scratching

Stroking

Inside a
Dog's Head

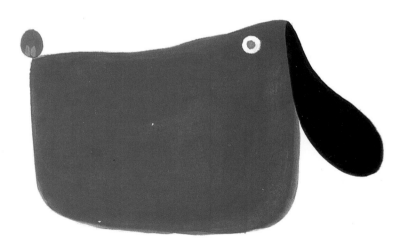

Noises I make…

Whimper

I'm scared.

It's a
dog
thing.

Happy

Casual

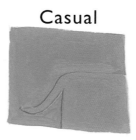

Alert

Worried

Chasing tails…

You would if you could.

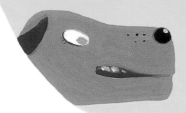

Eternal struggle...

...the mailman

Current affairs

extra

Bone
shares
rocket

I *do* watch TV.

I'm behind the sofa.

big sky dogs

Bad Things

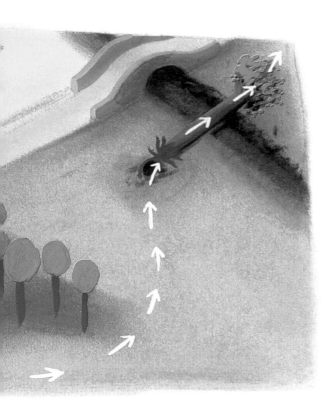

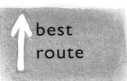

best
route

bully
dog's
house

Bully dog's teeth…

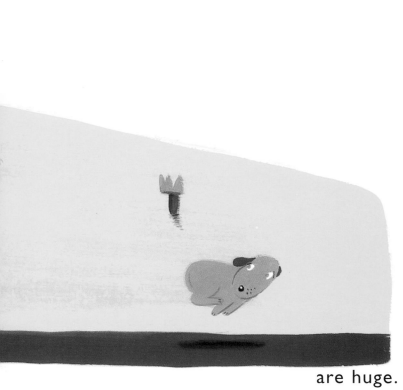

are huge.

Bath time

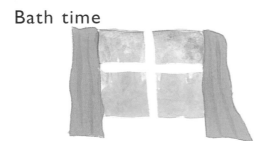

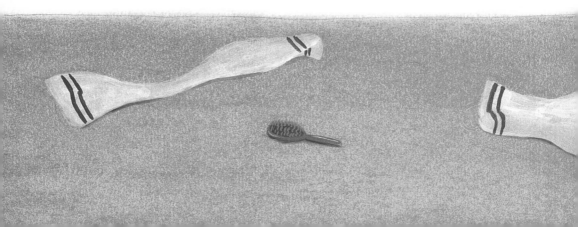

Fleas

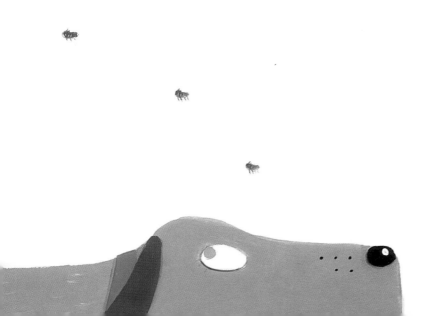

Those
things!

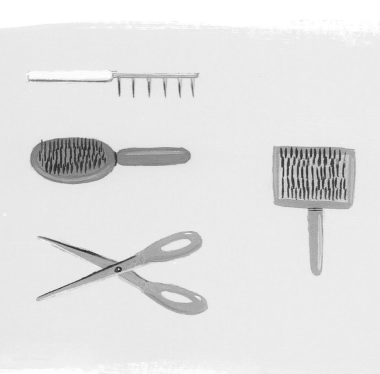

The vet...

I don't like it.

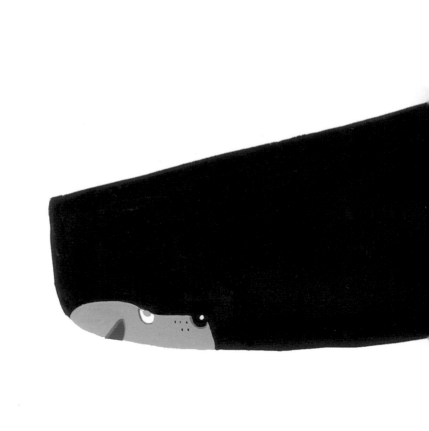

Cat claws

Fireworks

I think it's safe under

my blanket

Slippery floors

wipe out!

Dog
Dreams

action

Understudy for Lassie

"woof"

To be a St. Bernard

The first dog
in space

People food

yummy!

I'm top dog.

Climb like
a cat

What if it rained bones?

Call of the wild

The World

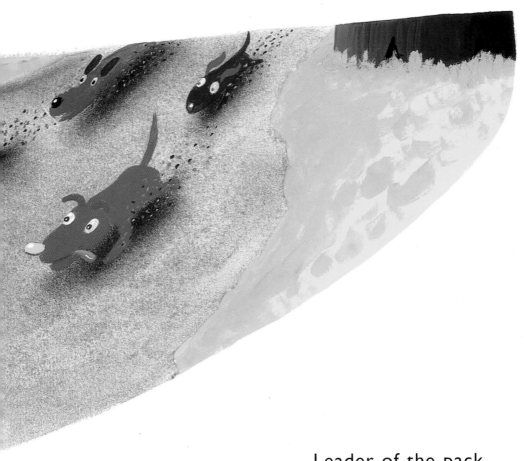

Leader of the pack

But best of
all is just being...

...a dog

About The Artist

Born in Yorkshire, James Croft studied in Cleveland, Leeds, and Wolverhampton and now lives in London. Sharing a flat with two college friends, three fish, a cactus, and numerous snails, James is frequently reminded of his rural upbringing which continues to influence his work.

First published in the United States in 2000 by
Laurel Glen Publishing
An imprint of the Advantage Publishers Group
5880 Oberlin Drive
San Diego, CA 92121-4794
www.advantagebooksonline.com

Publisher Allen Orso
Managing Editor JoAnn Padgett
Project Editor Elizabeth McNulty

Author/illustrator inquiries, and questions about permissions and rights should be
addressed to MQ Publications Ltd, 254–258 Goswell Road, London EC1V 7RL;
e-mail: mqp@btinternet.com

ISBN: 1-57145-656-2
Library of Congress Cataloging in Publication Data available upon request.

Printed in Italy

1 2 3 4 5   00 01 02 03 04